# Life *Change*

How change can be the best thing
that ever happened to you.

**GRAEME LAURIDSEN**

Copyright © 2018 Graeme Lauridsen

All rights reserved. No part of this publication may be reproduced, stored in a retrieval system, or transmitted, in any form or in any means – by electronic, mechanical, photocopying, recording or otherwise – without prior written permission.

ISBN: 978-0-9876394-0-0

Published by and all communication to:
www.graemelauridsen.com
2018

# About the Author

GRAEME LAURIDSEN IS the co-founder of COLAB Australia, a vibrant new company based in Melbourne, Australia, empowering leaders and business owners to reach their highest goals and achieve success.

After 30 years working with emerging leaders in the not-for-profit sector, he resigned from his position, sold everything, and embarked on a new career. It was a Life Change for both him and his family that would take many twists and turns, leading them to a new season of life and fulfilment.

Graeme now spends most of his time writing and speaking to business owners and leaders across Australia and New Zealand, mentoring many through their own Life Change journey. In doing so, many who have lost their passion, or find themselves trapped in mediocrity, are finding their true purpose in life, relationships, and career.

# CHAPTERS

About the Author .................................................................................iii

Chapter One:
Bored. Burnt Out. Frustrated. My story ...........................................1

Chapter Two:
Signs You Need to Transition ...........................................................5

Chapter Three:
Restlessness – When Not to Transition ..........................................13

Chapter Four:
Restoring Hope ................................................................................21

Chapter Five:
Transition What? .............................................................................27

Chapter Six:
Look Before You Leap ....................................................................35

Chapter Seven:
Leverage Everything .......................................................................41

Chapter Eight:
Keep Your Core Values- Change Your How Not Your Why .......45

Chapter Nine:
Surround the Vision with REST Resource ....................................53

Chapter Ten:
Surround the Vision with REST Ethos ..........................................59

Chapter Eleven:
Surround the Vision with REST Strategy .....................................69

Chapter Twelve:
Surround the Vision with REST Team ..........................................77

Epilogue:
Transition Versus Change ..............................................................81

## CHAPTER ONE
# Bored. Burnt Out. Frustrated. My story

MY WIFE AND I were sitting in a café with a close friend and mentor in a moment of crisis. We had been in our current role, leading a not-for-profit organisation, for almost fifteen years. The early years had been exciting. A difficult cashflow crisis had been averted, new team members had been added, vision had been refreshed, and there was growth and momentum on every side. However, the previous year had been extremely difficult. A crisis in our extended family had caused us stress and anxiety. Several leadership challenges and misunderstandings had drained us of our mental and emotional reserves, and some long-term relationships that were precious to us had come under considerable strain.

We all have those seasons. Most times we just press through. Life and leadership happen in cycles. Winter leads to spring, spring leads to summer, summer fades back to autumn, and autumn prepares us for another winter. These seasons build wisdom and maturity in our lives. We had been through a few cold winters, but we had always pressed through into spring and summer.

However, this time things felt different. There was one ingredient that had always been present that now seemed missing. We were finding it difficult to embrace that one thing that had always sustained us. We couldn't find hope!

Our close friend and mentor had flown into our city for the day with the sole purpose of encouraging us. He had heard that we were struggling and flew in to stand at our side. Let me quickly add that we all need those people in our life. An ancient proverb says, 'a friend loves at all times, and a brother is born for a time of adversity'. Thank God for the 'brothers' who are born for adversity. If you don't have one or two, the first step to getting one is to be one. Be someone else's brother who stands by their side in times of adversity. Some call it karma, but the truth is we reap what we sow; what we give to others tends to return in kind.

Our mentor began to ask us questions:

*How are you guys?*

*How is your health?*

*Are you struggling with stress or anxiety?*

*Are you still passionate about the work here?*

*Can you see things changing?*

*Do you have the energy to turn things around?*

He went deeper in asking my wife of her condition:

*How are you travelling?*

*Do you want to keep doing this?*

*How discouraged are you?*

*Is depression knocking on your door?*

After some time, he turned from his questions and made a statement; *Guys, I say this as a friend. I know how loyal you are, but I think your time is up. It's time to move on.*

My feelings were mixed at this suggestion. Half of me was struggling with the idea. I felt like I had unfinished business. My goals had not been fulfilled. There was much more that we wanted to achieve. Yet, at the same time, I felt a sense of relief. What if it was okay to step down? There were no guarantees that we could turn things around if we stayed. As a husband I needed to listen to the words my wife was speaking. What if my stubbornness caused her irreparable damage? Was it time?

Our friend flew out of the city at the end of the day, and we were left to process the conversation. One of the big questions we were asking was, what did moving on mean? I had been in the profession for twenty-five years. I was twenty-two years old when I first stepped into the not-for-profit sector, and I knew little else. We could move on and get another role in the same sector, but my heart was telling me that I needed a complete career transition. I was forty-seven years old, and I was considering a major career change!

To be honest, if I wasn't depressed already, this tipped me over. What could I do? How would I provide for my family? Would I find something that would give me a sense of achievement, of identity, of meaning?

We heard of a psychologist who specializes in helping people who are in burn-out, so we made an appointment for a meeting. His schedule was so full the only opportunity we had was to fly from the south of New Zealand to Adelaide, Australia, and attend a seminar he was speaking at. The organisers of the seminar were friends, and they managed to arrange one appointment for us.

We arrived in Adelaide, attended the seminar, filled out some forms, and turned up for our appointment. It wasn't long before this wise Irish psychologist was ready to offer his diagnosis. He looked me squarely in the eye and said words to this effect; *This season and environment is killing your wife, and you're not far behind. If you don't resign immediately, I fear you will be in complete burnout within three months.*

This book is about transition. Transition, as opposed to sudden change, is a process. It is a journey that is best taken slowly and methodically. It is like waking up one day, deciding you are out of shape, and putting an exercise and diet plan in place. It takes time and patience. However, we were not given the opportunity for a slow and steady transition. We had left it too late; the ambulance had been called and we were on the way to the emergency rooms. Drastic action needed to be taken.

We flew home, but now with two strong voices in our minds. The first was a friend and mentor suggesting our time was up, that it was time to move on. And now a psychologist advising us to take immediate action to escape an environment that had become unhealthy for us. We were facing a dilemma. We could take things slowly and risk our health and well-being, or we could resign immediately and risk unemployment and an uncertain future.

Two days later I gathered our board together and submitted my resignation. We leapt into the unknown. My wife immediately withdrew from the environment, and I undertook a succession process whereby I appointed my successor and ensured a smooth transition. We left with regrets. Relationships that were under strain through that difficult season never had time to heal before our departure. Dreams and goals were left unfulfilled. We had recently built our dream home and we had planned to live out our years there. It was a necessary decision that bought on a level of grief and sadness.

A few months later we had packed our belongings and left the city, heading to our home town a thousand kilometres to the north. Our transition had begun. Deep down, I knew that this was not only a geographical change. This was a major life and career transition.

Eight years have now passed as I write this chapter. I have fully and successfully transitioned from my previous role as a leader in the not-for-profit sector and an ordained minister, to an author, business and leadership mentor, and speaker. It has not been an easy journey. However, I have arrived at a destination that gives me great levels of satisfaction and hope for the future.

I now find myself meeting many fellow travellers who are trapped within a world where hope has departed. Many have suggested I document my journey as a roadmap for others to follow. For some time, I didn't feel the journey warranted my ability to share a roadmap, however I hope that after eight years I may have something helpful to share.

Welcome to *Life Change*.

CHAPTER TWO
# Signs You Need to Transition

**I**F I COULD do things over, what would I change? My primary regret is that I left things too late. There were signposts that I missed, or even ignored. Have you ever had a guest who has overstayed their welcome? I'm an early riser. When guests come for dinner, I wilt after 10.30pm. The problem is, I have friends who come alive at 10.30pm. I'm starting to fall asleep, but for them the party is only getting started.

I try to drop a few hints: maybe I take a few glances at my watch, an obvious yawn, or I change into my pyjamas! Perhaps I might curl up and fall asleep on the couch. Yes, I exaggerate. But you get the point. Sometimes we can stay too long in a place. Our creativity has dried up, our season is over, and we become stale.

So, what are the signs that we need to transition? Take a moment to look at the graphic below:

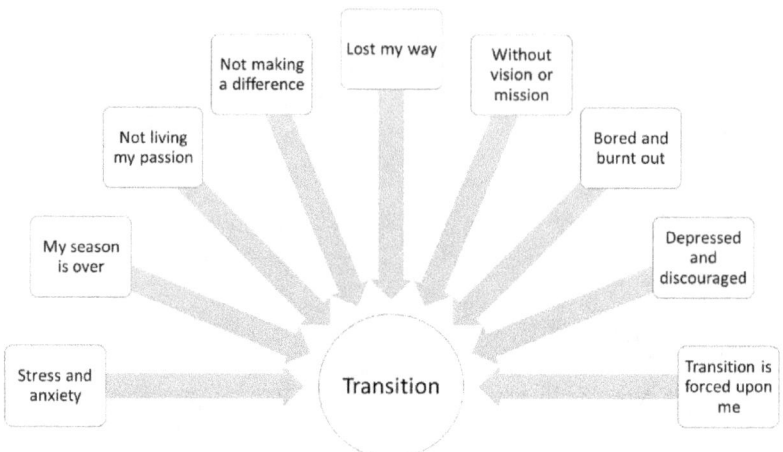

*Any of these symptoms can be a signpost that you need to transition.*

## 1. Stress and Anxiety

Being overcome by stress and anxiety is always a signpost that change is needed. At the very least a lifestyle change is required. We all experience stress at some level. We just cannot live there.

I mentioned in the opening chapter that we had experienced a crisis in our extended family. This crisis involved a very unfortunate chapter in my father's life that culminated in his arrest and eventual imprisonment. Without going into greater detail, my father did not respond well to his situation and lashed out aggressively against his family. For four years we walked through extreme crisis and conflict.

During this time, we also experienced greater than normal levels of stress within our workplace. To some degree, the two were related, however the outcome was that we were carrying unreasonable levels of stress and anxiety for too long.

My observation is that people in the *helping people* professions see stress and anxiety as an occupational hazard. They embrace a *martyr mentality* that keeps them going with a false sense of *taking one for the team*. The problem with this scenario is that we wouldn't treat animals the way we treat ourselves. We would never run a horse to exhaustion. In fact, if we did so, we would likely face criminal charges.

If you have been operating under stress and anxiety for extended periods of time, it may be a signpost that a transition is necessary. On its own it may only be a warning to change your lifestyle, however, if it is accompanied by several of the following symptoms, you may need to take more urgent attention:

## 2. Depressed and Discouraged

There can be many reasons why we experience discouragement and depression, but when they come together they can be a signpost to transition. Discouragement is a normal part of life. We have times when we make progress and are encouraged, and other times when we are not seeing progress and become discouraged. However, discouragement comes with a use-by date. It is unhealthy if it goes on too long. Discouragement that goes on for too long will eventually invite its room-mate, depression.

Sometimes the best thing we can do with discouragement is to change our game plan. Imagine that you have decided to be a competitive runner. You train for months and line up for your first 5k race. The starter gun sounds, and you begin the race. After a while you find that you are not keeping up. You keep trying, but the other runners soon disappear into the distance ahead of you. You finish the race in last place, just before the race organizers begin packing up to go home.

Of course, you go home a little discouraged. But you decide to keep training and try again. At the next race you repeat your first performance. Last again. As time goes on, the cycle continues. Running is just not your thing. Of course, if this was a movie, you would keep on trying and eventually win a gold medal at the Olympics. But this isn't the movies. If you don't eventually become encouraged with some progress, your discouragement can soon become depression. You could keep trying, and you may even pass a few runners, or you could take up another sport. It doesn't mean you cannot run for enjoyment, but if the goal is to win races, failure over an extended period can kill the joy.

Transitioning to a different goal can turn failure into success. I thought I was good at what I was doing. And for a long season, I was. For many years, we saw great fruitfulness and productivity. However, for us, that season came to an end. It wasn't anyone's fault. We don't look back needing to lay the blame somewhere. We simply stopped being productive. We could have decided to push through, but prolonged discouragement had turned to depression. I regret not seeing the signpost earlier.

## 3. Not Living Out My Passion

This was not a signpost to me; however, I am now meeting people regularly who are not living out their passion. My wife is an amazing woman. Of course, I do have great taste! The truth is, she was living out my passion, not hers. Being the 'supportive wife' meant quietly laying down her dreams to support mine. Often, life partners can co-exist with each one pursuing their own dreams, however we found that my role became all-consuming for both of us. She was drawn into my world in such a way that she could not find the room or freedom to follow her own dreams.

This was not intentional on our part, it just happened without our fully realizing the consequences. Over time she lost her passion for life and purpose. It was a signpost that we raced past without noticing. It was a missed signpost that I now live with, and with great regret.

Let me ask you a few questions:

*What do you really want to do with your life?*

*What difference do you want to make?*

*What gives you a sense of joy and accomplishment?*

*What replenishes your soul?*

If you are not living out your passion, I would suggest this is a clear signpost for you to consider a transition.

## 4. My Season is Over

Sometimes, if we turn down the noise in our life, we just know. There will be people reading this chapter who deep down know the game is over. In fact it may have been over for a long time. It may be that the risk of transition is too great. You have become comfortable with the safe and the secure. Better the devil you know than the devil you don't. What if you fail in the transition? I would reply, what if you succeed?

The danger is one day you might find it is too late to change. I was 47 years old when I went back to school to finish my management degree. I was 55 years old when I was confident that I had transitioned into a new and radically different season. If you suspect your season is over, at least explore your options.

## 5. Bored and Burnt Out

Boredom is a great wake-up call. I remember in our meeting with the psychologist, that he said to me, "You have become stale!" At the time I didn't believe him. I was a charismatic leader and speaker and well regarded among my peers. However, he was right. Not only was I burnt-out, I was bored. I needed new air to breathe. I needed new challenges. I needed fresh adventures.

## 6. Without Vision or Mission

It is my personal belief that each one of us are born with a deep sense of purpose and mission. Often, in my business coaching role, I ask people; "If there is a God in Heaven who put you on the planet to solve one problem, what would that problem be?" I am amazed at how often I receive profound replies. Let me ask you a similar question; What is your dream? If you could achieve anything in your life for others, what would you attempt?

Are you actively involved in the pursuit of that dream? If not, what are you waiting for? For some, this signpost is linked to your season being over. Perhaps for many years you could articulate your vision for the future, but now you struggle. If you have lost your vision, either get it back, or consider a transition.

## 7. Not Making a Difference

This signpost is like the previous one. Most people want to make a difference. If that's not you, you can probably stop reading. (Thanks for getting this far.) But if you have a deep desire to make a difference, to be remembered, to leave a legacy, and you are not living out that desire, it may be that you are ready for a transition.

I believe that you exist to make a difference. Your life should count. Your transition may even be a minor one. Instead of changing your life and career, you might add to it. It may be as simple as volunteering at your local church or charity. It may be helping in a homeless shelter. Whatever you do, if you are not making a difference, transition.

## 8. When Transition is Forced on You

There are also times when change is not a choice. In 1987, my wife returned home to find that her first husband had died. In a moment her life changed. Her future hopes and expectations were radically altered. The transition she faced was not of her own choice. It was thrust upon her and she had no alternative but to navigate through to a new season.

I am sure we could all share dozens of stories of our own and of others we know, who have had transition forced upon them. From being made redundant in the workplace, to sickness, to the loss of a loved one, to an untimely marriage breakdown; transition can visit us unexpectedly.

## 9. Lost My Way

For some, you have simply lost your way. Perhaps you missed a signpost and you feel lost. Many people feel this way. The good news is feeling lost is the beginning of your journey home. It is a signpost in and of itself. Embrace the rest of this book as your roadmap to purpose.

Your transition begins here.

CHAPTER THREE
# Restlessness – When Not to Transition

MANY YEARS AGO I had a boss who would talk about transition in three stages: restlessness, vision, advance. It was his belief that the first stage of transition was restlessness.

I'm sure this can be true; however, restlessness can also be a reason not to transition. Some people have restless souls. If this is the case, restlessness can be a false signpost. Personally, I have a restless soul. I like change. I get bored easily. But I have had to learn early that my restlessness is not necessarily a signpost to change.

I include this chapter as a safeguard for the restless. Before you use your restlessness as a reason for transition, I would like to give you five reasons restlessness could be a false signpost.

## 1. Restlessness as a Sign of Discontentment

Restlessness can be a sign that the problem is within ourselves, as opposed to our external environment. If such is the case, a transition will only be a short-term remedy. One of the heroes of the Bible is the apostle Paul. He was responsible for writing a sizable portion of the New Testament. Much of his time was spent travelling, starting new churches, and being arrested!

He makes this observation:

> *I know what it is to be in need, and I know what it is to have plenty. I have learned the secret of being content in any and every situation, whether well fed or hungry, whether living in plenty or in want.*
>
> Philippians 4:12 (New International Version)

Sometimes restlessness can be a signpost that we need to learn the secret of being content in any and every situation. Discontentment can be a learned condition that is more a sign of immaturity than a need for change.

Have you ever seen a child who is never satisfied? No matter what they have, they want something else. They have a short attention span and are always looking for 'the next thing'. Part of growing up is learning to be content with what you have. This does not take away our drive for success, rather that we can also be at peace in our current circumstances.

Be careful that restlessness born of discontentment does not become a signpost for constant change. The best antidote for discontentment is to develop a habit of thankfulness. Begin every day being thankful for what you have, for who is in your life, for the world in which you live. Be thankful for the car you drive, the roof over your head, the family surrounding you, and the friends who care for you. Constant thankfulness will protect you from the restlessness born of discontentment.

## 2. Restlessness from a Lack of Perseverance and Tenacity

Another reason not to transition is when the going gets tough. You may remember the song by Kenny Rogers called *The Gambler*.

*You got to know when to hold 'em, know when to fold 'em,*

*Know when to walk away and know when to run.*

ONE OF THE businesses I work closely with has taken on some very large projects. The CEO and founder of the company will often meet with the staff to inspire and equip them for their roles. On one occasion he painted a picture of the mountain before them. "Over the next year, we will climb this mountain. It will mean all hands on deck. It will be a big challenge. But then we will be on the other side, and we will enjoy the rewards."

It was an extremely challenging year. The entire staff went the extra mile and the project was completed and the rewards were shared.

Quitting half way up the mountain would have meant the loss of great rewards. Sometimes the going gets tough. We need to know when to hold 'em, and know when to fold 'em. There have been many times when our best option was perseverance and tenacity. However, there also came a time when we needed to fold 'em, to know when to walk away, and when to run. Wisdom is knowing the difference.

How do we know when to press through with perseverance and tenacity, and when to transition? Let me make two observations:

First, we need to know that choosing transition can be more difficult than staying. If you are planning a transition to escape the need for perseverance and tenacity, you will be disappointed. To transition well, you will need all the perseverance and tenacity you can muster. Transition is not necessarily the easier option. It is not an escape from the need for perseverance, but a pathway into it.

Second, there is an old proverb that says, 'in the multitude of counsellors there is safety'. Get advice from the right people. Without the counsel of both professionals and friends we would not have moved. There were some who advised us to stay, but in the full body of counsel we received the weight of advice convinced us that our issue was not a lack of perseverance but a time to transition.

## 3. Restlessness as a Sign of Personal Frustration

Sometimes we struggle to like ourselves. We are frustrated with who we are, and we mistakenly believe that if we change our circumstances, we will change our mood. One of my favourite bands is *Crowded House*. The lyrics to one of their most popular songs say, 'Everywhere you go you always take the weather with you'.

If your transition is born of a personal struggle with yourself, here is the sad news: everywhere you go, you take yourself with you. A change of scenery will not change the weather, or how you feel about yourself. It may come as no surprise to you, but most people struggle with self-esteem. Have you noticed how almost everyone on Facebook paints a perfect picture of themselves? They find their best moments and their best photos, and post the ideal life. Why do we tend to do this? Because we desperately want to be accepted. We want people to know that we are successful, loved and happy.

Most people want to portray the image that they could be cast in one of those *coca cola* ads. The truth is this often masks a real world of pain and personal disappointment.

Don't transition because of personal frustration. I have mentioned the difficult chapter we experienced with my father. In all honesty, our relationship was never an easy one. My dad was haunted by his own demons, and his frustration was often vented upon those closest to him. As a small child, I can remember the words spoken in his anger. I was 'good for nothing and would never amount to anything. I was useless, and if he wanted a job done, he would be better to do it himself than get me to help'. Remember, these were his words to a child, not an adult.

I grew with these words echoing in my soul. I left school early. My first job lasted five months. My second, nine months. My third, five months. My fourth, three months. And on the cycle continued.

I am not a counsellor or psychologist, but I do have a story. How do you heal a wounded soul? We are often a reflection of how those closest to us perceive us. I became a reflection of my father's words. However, I couldn't keep transitioning to escape my own low self-esteem. I would eventually need to face the music.

How do we do that? I share this as an alternative to transition if your transition is born of personal frustration. My father created a soundtrack that was accompanying my journey. I chose to do two things.

First, I chose to forgive. If I held a grudge, that soundtrack would echo in my soul forever. It seems such an irony that unforgiveness is like taking a capsule of poison and hoping the other person dies. If a significant person has written a soundtrack of negativity and abuse into your life, please consider forgiving them and letting it go – not for their benefit, but for yours. By forgiving them you take away their power to hold you captive.

Second, I decided to find a new sound track. I needed a new narrative. I needed new words to describe who I am. Where you find that narrative is entirely up to you. As for me, I found that narrative through embracing a personal faith. Some reading this book may see this as a weakness, but for me, it was my new strength. To fully believe that there is a loving God in Heaven who invites us to call him Father made a difference. To find that I was born with meaning and purpose changed everything.

Go find your new positive narrative. This may include building positive people into your social circle, reading some of the great books that have been written about building positivity into your life, or the art of self-talk – changing the narrative yourself.

However your journey unfolds, be careful that restlessness born of frustration doesn't become your signpost for transition. Find a new narrative that can build your self-esteem.

## 4. Restlessness as an Escape from Difficult Circumstances

Sometimes our circumstances are difficult. For example, our relationships go through challenges. These are not always a good reason to transition. In the early days of our transition, I was miserable. I was angry at life, I was angry at God, and I was terribly discouraged. I doubt that I was easy to live with.

Perhaps my only point here is that I am glad that my wife didn't decide that my pain was reason for her to transition. We came through together.

If you are considering a transition, first consider whether your circumstances can change without the transition. Ask the question, will this season pass with some wise counsel and time? Sometimes it is better to fight through to a better season.

## 5. Restlessness that Unsettles Our Loved Ones

Finally, before we let restlessness dictate a transition, our loved ones need to be considered. In our previous chapter we explored the various signs that a transition may be necessary. In this chapter we have looked at the opposing argument. What are the reasons for when we should consider pressing on? One consideration is the effect a transition could have on our loved ones.

We may have a partner in a successful career, or children settled in school, or a transition may mean our loved ones will need to leave friends and family.

To my shame, early in my life *I followed my passion*, often at the cost of my loved ones. At the time I fully believed I was *following my calling*, so it was therefore justified. I was wrong! We moved when my wife would have preferred to have stayed. She never complained, and I was often oblivious, as she is not a *words person*. She may comment once, but then she will leave it.

Hindsight is a wonderful thing. Isn't it strange that we take a lifetime to learn how to live a life! Let me be brutally honest, not as an act of humility, but to share some advice and hopefully save someone from unnecessary pain. If I had my time over again, I would sacrifice more for my family. I would ask more questions and listen more to the answers. Before you transition – consider the cost to those closest to you.

We have now looked at why we shouldn't transition. For us, the choice to transition outweighed the reasons not to. The symptoms

## Chapter Three: Restlessness – When Not to Transition

created a signpost that was too clear to ignore. And we have no regrets. I wouldn't trade my new life for my old, yet at the same time, I don't regret the life we had. It was simply time for a change.

If, like us, you are still considering a transition, the following chapters will be more practical. I will share our roadmap. We ventured into uncharted territory without a guide. I am sure there are resources out there that would have been helpful, we just didn't find them in time.

A radical transition like ours is not easy. In fact there were moments we felt it was impossible. But the rewards when we arrived were worth the cost.

# CHAPTER FOUR
# Restoring Hope

IT MAY BE that you have made the decision that something needs to change. You are ready to move on to the next chapter of your life. Where do you begin? What comes first? You may remember that the one component that signalled our transition was the absence of hope. Hope is like oxygen to the soul. When hope is lost, our first step is always to find it again. Of course, the opposite of hope is hopelessness. If that is where you find yourself, then to restore hope it is important you understand something about the nature of hopelessness.

## Hopelessness is Deceptive

Hopelessness is like an unwelcome guest who doesn't want to leave. In its attempt to make your world its permanent home, it tries to sell you a lie. What is the lie? That 'this is as good as it gets'. The nature of hopelessness is the idea that there is nothing worth hoping for; the idea that things cannot and will not get better. It is at this point that we need to begin our transition. Imperative to your moving forward is to regain the strongly held belief that there is hope. I have no doubt that there will be some reading this chapter who will find this hard to receive. You have become so enveloped by hopelessness that you are beginning to believe the lie. I understand, and I have been there. But I have lived to tell the tale.

> There is no such thing as hopelessness! (Yes, you read that right.) There is always hope.

The real question is not whether hope exists, but where do we find it? The answer to that question is that we often find it outside our current worldview. To do that, we need to understand a second point about the nature of hopelessness;

## Hopelessness is Territorial

In other words, hopelessness lives within a narrow context. Perhaps we can explain it this way; imagine you are locked inside an empty warehouse with no food or water. To your knowledge, every door is locked and there is no way out. As a few days pass, you begin to lose hope. If you don't get water soon, life will be over, and as time goes on with no rescue, hopelessness settles in.

There is no hope because there is no food or water within the context of the warehouse. Of course, beyond the warehouse there is an abundance of food and water. There is a MacDonald's restaurant and a supermarket only a few miles away. If you could reach beyond the warehouse, hope would be restored. Our challenge is to reach beyond our warehouse, and to believe that there is hope beyond the context of our current worldview where we will find food and water in abundance.

In our situation, we had been living within a career context for twenty-five years. Our work and lifestyle were like being locked inside the warehouse. It was where my reputation and credibility lived. It was where we felt confident, and where future opportunities would come from. What made things even more difficult is I felt a sense of calling to that world. That sense of calling locked me inside the warehouse.

I was losing hope because I believed my only future was within that context. And hopelessness began to lie by telling me that 'this is as good as it gets'.

Let me say this, there is a big world beyond your current context. There are other places to work. There are other careers. There are other towns, cities, and even countries that would welcome you. There are good people you have not yet met who will believe in you. To regain hope you may need to look outside the square. Are there other options? Is there something else you would love to do? Can you do the same thing, but somewhere else? There are always options beyond your current context.

## Thinking Outside the Box

The first step in restoring hope is to identify the box. The box is the context within which you believe you should live. It could be geographical. It could be within a career, or an industry, it could even be relational (but please do not use this concept as an excuse to move on from your significant relationships). If you are looking at a transition, it is possible that the box is causing you to experience hopelessness. So, what is your current box? Begin by answering the following questions.

## Is the Box Your Career?

Sometimes our transition is a change of career. My wife is a registered nurse. She is highly qualified and can find work anywhere. Nursing was her safe place that provided financial security. However, to find hope and purpose, she recognised it would most likely be found outside the nursing box. Is it your career that is holding you captive?

## Is the Box Geographical?

Perhaps you need a change of scenery. I have met many people along the way who have taken the risk and shifted location. One of the interesting things about geographical boxes is that transitions can be temporary. I could share dozens of stories of people who have moved to foreign countries or faraway cities for a few years and have fond memories and made life-long friends. They often return, but the temporary transition reinvigorated their world and enabled them to disengage from the treadmill. Consider whether your location is the box that you need to think beyond.

## Is the Box Relational?

It could be that you have been working with the same people for too long. This could mean management or co-workers. Sometimes we just get bored. However, if your relationships have become the box that is holding you captive, remember that your next relationships may not improve your world. But then again, they just might.

The first step in restoring hope is to look beyond your current context. The world you see now may only be a small part of a much bigger picture. There are opportunities beyond your current perspective that, if you saw them, would fill you with hope and anticipation.

I have a brother by the name of Terry. He is a year older than me, and we grew up as good friends. Of course, we fought like brothers do, but we had many adventures together. In his early twenties, Terry lost his way. He began to experiment with drugs, and the experiments turned into an addiction. He married, but the marriage failed within months. He began to fall into depression and, because of his addiction, struggled to control his anger.

He developed a relationship with a new partner, and after a few volatile years the relationship came to an end. In Terry's mind, all hope was gone; his life was one failure after another. Hopelessness coaxed him into the belief that things would never get better. Hopelessness also convinced him that he was trapped in a small world, that there were no options, there were no new careers, no professional help for his addictions, no future relationships, and no hope of happiness to come. As you may suspect, on the 20$^{th}$ November 1987, Terry made the permanent and irreversible decision to end his life. Today he would have been 56 years old. He died not being able to see beyond the context of his current circumstances.

Remember this statement: *There is no such thing as hopelessness.* Hopelessness is a feeling, not a truth. There is always hope. Sometimes it is further on the horizon than you can currently see, or just around a corner that you are yet to turn.

## CHAPTER FIVE
# Transition What?

Before we talk about a transition plan, it is worth getting a little more focussed on what part of your life is in need of a transition. One of the biblical parables speaks of a young man who got impatient waiting for his father's inheritance. Bored and frustrated from working on the family farm, he convinced his father to give him his share of the family inheritance early, so he could go and live a life of his own desires. As the story unfolds, the young man wastes the entire inheritance on wild living until eventually he is trapped in a life of poverty and shame.

Of course, the original narrative is about the love of his father in receiving him home, but in our context another question is worth asking. Instead of 'transitioning everything', could he have 'transitioned something'? He was most likely a well-educated young man from a wealthy family. Perhaps he was bored and restless. He was the second son, so it was most likely that the elder brother would inherit the farm, so his future was unclear. What other options were available to him that would not have meant losing everything?

Perhaps a gap year was all that he needed. His father would likely have financed a year of travelling without dipping into the inheritance. Alternatively, going to a university to study could have set him up for his future. He could have learnt a trade in the town nearby, made a new set of friends, taken up mountain climbing, become involved in politics, or any other number of 'transitions' that would not have risked his entire inheritance.

The danger of making a 'Life Change' is that we can inadvertently 'transition everything' when we only needed to 'transition something'. One way we can address this dilemma is to create two lists, one headed *things I am willing or need to change*, and another *things to keep*. For example, the wayward son in the parable would have been well served if on his *things to keep* list he wrote *my inheritance*, and *my relationship with my father*. If those two keepers were his priority, he would likely have saved himself immense heartache and misfortune.

On the next page there is a template of the two lists. By completing this exercise, I hope you will find yourself growing in hope and confidence for a better future. It marks the beginning of your transition plan. It will bring some clarity to what you are ready to change, and what you need to keep as a foundation upon which to build your new future.

## Chapter Five: Transition What?

| Things I am willing or need to change. | Things to keep. |
|---|---|
|  |  |

Let's begin with the second column. What areas of your life are not open to transition? These are your keepers.

What are some examples that you may write in this column?

## Family and Close Friends

Sometimes a transition may mean moving away from family and friends. This may not mean deciding against a transition, but rather that maintaining relationships is non-negotiable. Our transition meant moving countries. This meant leaving our elderly parents behind. Because 'family' was on our *things to keep* list, we needed to adopt a plan to maintain contact. Part of the budget included regular flights home, skype sessions, social media, and communication. If you don't write family and friends into your *things to keep* list, and make maintaining these relationships intentional, you may be surprised how quickly you lose contact.

As our parents became unwell, we needed to seriously consider whether it was time to 'transition back home' because they were firmly on our *things to keep* list.

## Superannuation/Retirement Savings

Many have made the decision to 'cash in' their retirement savings to invest in a new business enterprise. This is gambling your future financial security on the present. Of course, if the gamble pays off, you will have no regrets. However, I would first ask this question. Is there another way? Is there an alternative plan? It is your decision whether your retirement savings should go on your *things to keep* list. I would only suggest that you need a good reason for it not to.

## Career

Some people would put career on their list. I mentioned earlier that my wife transitioned from her nursing career. However, I should also add that for many years she maintained her practising certificate. Her career was placed on hold as she pursued other opportunities, but it was too valuable to sacrifice completely before she had found financial security in her new season.

## Location

Obviously, location didn't make it to our *things to keep* list, however for many it might. There are many reasons a person may choose to transition only within their geographical location. It may be their partner's career, or family and friends, or even lifestyle. It is by filling in your *things to keep* list that you narrow the focus on what your future transition will look like. It narrows the options. It also creates a level of stability in your world, as 'not everything is going to change'.

## Purpose and Values

This may seem obvious, but it is more important than we might first think. Even though I was changing career, I didn't want to change my life purpose or personal values. For example, I could have transitioned to a quiet beachside area and mowed lawns for absent home-owners. At the time it was tempting, however the boredom would have destroyed me. I have always had a passion to empower people to embrace their most extraordinary life. Whatever future role I embraced, I wanted to make a difference to people. Second, I didn't want to abandon my deeply held beliefs. I wanted my values to be the solid ground upon which I embarked on a major transition. My faith would stay the same. Integrity would remain my goal. Generosity would continue to be my discipline. I have always desired to embrace an attitude of humility and forgiveness, not holding a grudge, and treating others as I would hope to be treated. These were my keepers!

Before you finish, invite loved ones to be involved as you write in this column. Your partner and children need a voice. Of course, sometimes our children don't have the wisdom to make these decisions, and they may never want to leave their friends, but the conversation now will be much easier than picking up the pieces later. Give them a voice on the journey.

Now consider the first list.

Let's ask the question, 'what am I willing to change, or need to change?' This is the time to be honest. I 'needed' to change my job. I could have taken a sabbatical. My board would likely have given us a year to replenish; they were generous and considerate. But deep down, I knew it would only delay the inevitable.

Be honest with yourself. What do you need to change? Career? Location? Who you hang out with?

Sometimes a transition may simply, or also, be around your health. You may decide that your transition is from being overweight and unfit to health and wellness. That is your 'need to change' decision. However, your success will also be dependent upon what you are willing to change.

Are you willing to change your lifestyle, your diet, your alcohol consumption, or your daily routines and disciplines?

My list looked a little like this:

| Things I am willing or need to change. | Things to keep. |
|---|---|
| Need to change:<br>Career.<br>High pressure lifestyle.<br>Physical health.<br>How I support my family's dreams.<br><br>Willing to change:<br>Location.<br>Skills and Qualifications.<br>Routines.<br>The need to live in our own home. | My marriage.<br>Our retirement plan.<br>Family connections.<br>Close friends and mentors.<br>My core life purpose of helping and empowering people.<br>My core values of faith, integrity, generosity, humility, and forgiveness. |

CHAPTER SIX
# Look Before You Leap

THE BEGINNING OF any *Life Change* journey is to first consider where the next destination might be. If you were to make the decision to transition, where would you transition to? What could your future look like?

If you were to jump into your car and take a drive with no destination in mind, you wouldn't be going anywhere in particular, you would only be taking a drive. The old adage applies, aim at nothing and you are sure to hit it.

Of course, if you are transitioning because of burnout, having a new vision is easier said than done. We were not healthy enough to dream again. Our transition was at first more about leaving an unhealthy environment than running to a new one. We were escaping!

However, over time, we did begin to dream again. We did need to type a new destination into the GPS. This wasn't easy, but we had to look before we leapt. In this chapter, I would like to share some thoughts on how to set a new direction when you have decided to transition. Let's assume that you don't have a clear picture of the future yet. Like us, you only know that you need to change. Where do you start?

## 1. Become a No Pressure Zone

Sometimes you don't know, and it's okay to get comfortable with that uncertainty. That is a good place to begin. Deciding to transition is enough of an effort in and of itself. Personally, I found this difficult. I am one of those people who like to have the future planned out. Often, when I was speaking at a conference, I would be introduced as a contagious visionary. Having no vision was torture. But I needed to embrace that reality and become comfortable with it. Get over the guilt of having no vision. It is not a permanent condition. There are times we need to remember how to 'be' and not be wrapped up in our 'do'. Remember, we are first and foremost human beings, not human doings.

Be okay with not knowing. Live in the in-between for a while.

## 2. Begin to Dream Again

Learn to dream outside of the box. Earlier we shared about being trapped inside a context. Begin to dream about what your life could look like in a different context. Ask questions like, what other careers could I see myself embracing? What could life look like in a different location? Have I had other dreams that I never pursued? If nothing were impossible, what would I attempt?

## 3. Connect with Your Deep Why

Most times when we transition, we change our what, not our why. I mentioned in the last chapter that my core life purpose was placed firmly in my things to keep column. Transitioning is to reconnect with our deep why, and yet possibly placing it inside a different context. For example, I have not transitioned from what I believe is my life purpose and passion. From my youngest memories I have always loved helping others to be successful. I would help others in my class at school who were struggling with their work.

My career has been spent teaching and inspiring others to live both purposefully and successfully. My personal purpose statement is to 'empower others to live an extraordinary life'. I took my why, and placed it inside the business world. On the outside many would assume that I am living in a very different world today however, on the inside, I am fulfilling the same passion. I'm still helping people embrace and live their most extraordinary life.

## 4. What Are Your Options?

Begin to write down all the different options. What are the possibilities before you? Consider different career options, owning your own business, or even a geographical shift. In our situation, we understood that anything was possible, but there were specific options before us.

We could return to our home town, which initially we did. I could apply for some low stress jobs to see me through the transition. I applied for lots. We could take a year's sabbatical, maybe pick fruit on farms or live near the beach, which for a few months we did. We could retrain and get new qualifications, which we both did.

We could talk to friends and acquaintances and let them know that we are looking for new opportunities. On that note, it is always wise to be nice to people on life's journey. Treat everyone like they are your boss, as one day they might be!

## 5. Play the Long Game

When you are in transition, be careful not to rush. Play the long game. It took us seven years to work through the four steps above. Take a moment to consider that thought. I was 48 years old when we decided to transition. I was 55 when we figured out what our best options were. That gave me around 15 years of career left. Take your time to dream again.

## 6. See the End Goal and Work Your Way Back

Once you have a clear picture of what you are transitioning to, paint a picture of the end goal. For example, I asked myself, when I am 70, what do I see? Could you write down a detailed description of what you would like your life to look like next? I wrote this:

*"I will be helping hundreds of thousands of people across the world embrace and live their most extraordinary life. I will be a seasoned and skilled business and leadership coach; I will be known for the books I write. I will build a global network of people with a similar passion, and I will be a valued keynote speaker bringing life and hope to people who are courageous enough to embrace transition."*

It took me a number of years to draw that picture, and I am sure it will take many more to see it fully come to pass.

## 7. Work Your Way Back

Once you see the end game, there are several questions to ask. What could I achieve in the next year? What could I achieve in five years? What could I achieve in ten years? Build your milestones towards your end goal.

In my first year, I set several goals that would prepare me for the future:

- Complete my management degree
- Begin to write some of the wisdom principles that I would continue to develop over the future. I established a life and leadership model called the REST model, which has become the foundation of much of my work
- Sell our home and put funds aside for future investment
- Write a business plan around future investment and wealth creation
- Establish ourselves in a new location

My five-year plan was:

- Establish myself as a voice of wisdom in the marketplace

- Build a network of connections in the business sector who have common values and goals
- Get as much experience in offering business support and coaching as possible
- Establish an online presence as a mentor and coach
- Write and release a book outlining a model for successful leadership

As I pursued these goals I found a business leader who was already doing many of the things I wanted to do. I didn't need to reinvent the world. I made an appointment and asked how I could serve his vision. To begin with I helped arrange the chairs in his training room. I attended every meeting he spoke at. I leaned in, took notes, and learnt as much as I could. I tried to be the first to arrive, and the last to leave.

One day he asked if I would speak for a few minutes at one of his seminars. Things went well. He then asked me to take a 20-minute session. Again, I more than survived. Over a few years of serving his vision, he invited me to be a business coach within his fast-growing, shared office space and business centres.

The more I planned and pursued the dream, the more opportunities came my way. A business school needed someone who could refresh and rejuvenate their vision and strategies. One could say that I was in the right place at the right time. Another view is that I had already been there in my mind.

# CHAPTER SEVEN
# Leverage Everything

One of the mistakes we can make in transition is to press factory reset. Most people who know me know that I am a complete novice when it comes to technology. Recently I was so frustrated with my mobile phone that I did a factory reset. Everything I had stored on the phone was lost. All my contacts, photos, addresses – you get the picture.

I was even more frustrated.

Someone asked why I didn't back up my phone before doing the reset. He nearly wore the phone!

All the contacts I had gathered over many years, all the photos, all the data, the memos, they were all gone. I would have to start again.

Here's the point. When we transition, every experience, every qualification, every relationship, in fact your whole life story until now is leverage upon which to build your future. You don't have to start again. Leverage everything. We do this by asking several questions:

## 1. What Qualifications and Experience Can Be Transferred To My New Season?

Remember, I was a 48-year-old leaving the not-for-profit sector with a desire to become a voice of wisdom in the business sector. Starting again at the age of 48 is a big ask, therefore I had to reconsider my viewpoint. I didn't need to start again. I had thirty years of experience to draw from. I simply needed to understand how I could leverage that experience.

Many years before our transition I had started a business degree that was never completed. I could complete the degree and leverage the qualification in the future. By doing so I became someone with a Bachelor of Applied Management with a double major in entrepreneurship and strategic management. That's leverage.

I have always had an interest in property investment. Over the years we had purchased, renovated, developed, or owned over thirty properties. We leveraged that experience and became directors of our own property investment company. We were beginning to build a new persona that would give us credibility in our new season.

In my career journey I have been privileged to be invited to speak at churches, schools, conferences and charities in and across New Zealand, Australia, the Pacific Islands, Indonesia, Cambodia, Malaysia, Singapore, and the United Kingdom. I have spoken on almost 5000 occasions to groups as small as 20 to as large as 2,500. I was an international speaker. That's leverage!

What qualifications and experience can you draw upon from your past to help position you for your future?

## 2. Who Might Help Me?

In a time of transition, people can be your greatest resource. Do you know someone who has already experienced a similar transition? Are there people you know who are already in the space that you could transition into? Who can you ask for advice and support? Who could provide a reference for you? Can an acquaintance provide you with temporary employment while you pass through the transition?

You may be uncomfortable using people as leverage, however friends exist for such a time. Most people who know you are more than happy to help you if they can.

It was people who made our transition successful, and we will be forever grateful. Here are just a few of the examples:

The wonderful real estate friend who helped us sell our home.

The family friend who needed a house sitter at just the right time for us to stay for a month.

The friends who had a beach chalet that allowed us to stay without charge for a few months. We experienced great friendship and memories over that time.

The old friend who connected us with a psychologist who specializes in stress and burnout recovery. We are forever grateful for his help.

The friend who offered us a job for one year as we walked through our transition. We were able to help with his temporary need, and he was able to give us a safe place to replenish.

The many friends who gave us counsel along the way.

Friends who gave us a reference for a house to rent.

This list could go on. I could add that people helped and invested in us as even though we had our share of failures. Not every path we ventured along was a success, but so many people graciously stood with us.

They were part of our leverage into a new season.

Consider the different relationships you can draw from during your transition.

## 3. What Resources Can I Leverage?

One of the greatest challenges we face in a significant transition is the financial burden. In our situation, we resigned without first securing future employment. We also chose to sell our home during a financial downturn. We were in the middle of the Global Financial Crisis of 2010. This meant discounting our home by hundreds of thousands of dollars to get a sale.

All of this meant that we were entering a new and uncertain future with limited resources and meagre savings.

The question we had to ask was, how do we best leverage our limited resources to get through this transition?

We have seen many people fail to fully think this through. Instead of leveraging their resources, they have lived off them without a secure plan. Eventually the money runs out and that great enemy called hopelessness comes knocking on their door.

Instead of living off our leftover funds, we chose to invest what little we had in a property. I spent many days and nights painting and repairing this broken-down property to add further value. I would then leverage the increase in value to buy another broken down property, and the cycle of hard work would continue. There would be numerous times when we had moved to Australia that I would fly back to New Zealand for a few weeks, sleep on the floor of a new house, repair and paint from the moment I woke until I would lie down to sleep at night. Each time I would increase the value of the property enough to use as leverage to invest in the next one.

After five years of renting a home to live in, and leveraging our resources, we had gained enough funds to build our own home, and then after seven years, we had increased our resources enough to launch a new Pilates studio, paying the first year's expenses in advance.

Leveraging your resources is not as simple as it might sound. The key is to get advice. Find a trustworthy advisor who can help you protect what you have, while at the same time gaining increase over time.

## CHAPTER EIGHT
# Keep Your Core Values- Change Your How Not Your Why

As I have already mentioned, most times transition is more external than internal. My 'why', or deeper purpose in life, stayed the same, however, 'how' I fulfilled that purpose changed.

The first step we take when helping guide someone through their Life Change is what we call a 'life audit'. We ask questions like: Why are you in transition? Where are you in life now? How did you get here? What are your regrets? What opportunities have been missed? What mistakes have been made? What risks have not been taken?

We ask them to describe their ideal life and consider the obstacles in embracing that life. We ask them what they would change about their life if they had the power to do so. Finally, we ask how they would like to be remembered. Consider this question: If there was one problem in this world that you were born to solve, what would it be?

Being able to answer such a question will give us the ability to reach deep into the core of our 'life purpose' and provide us with a steady anchor through times of change.

I believe that my purpose on Earth is to solve the problem of hopelessness and discouragement. I have a deep belief that human beings have the power to live extraordinary lives. I see potential in everyone I meet, and I am driven to help empower people to live to and fulfil that potential.

My hope is that we would die without potential. Nobody wants it said at their funeral that they had real potential. No. Better that people say we lived up to our potential, that we fought our fight, that we finished our race, and that we left nothing in the tank at the end of race day. Potential is God's gift to us. Fulfilling our potential is our gift back to Him.

That is my core. It was my core before I transitioned, and it remains my core today. I changed my *how*, not my *why*.

So, let me ask you: What is your core? What is the problem you exist to solve? What is the solution you bring to life's table? Let's establish your core before we plan your transition.

Perhaps now would be the time to introduce you to the REST model that forms the foundation of our Life Change programme. In the graphic below you will see what looks like the sights of a rifle. At the very centre of the graphic is the word *vision*. *Vision* includes a description of your 'deep why'. It is having a clear picture of what you would like to achieve in your lifetime. Around *vision* you will see four sectors resource, ethos, strategy, and team.

Chapter Eight: Keep Your Core Values- Change Your How Not Your Why

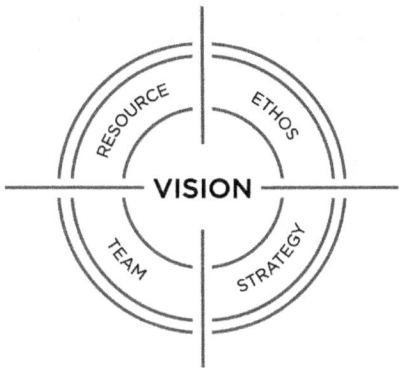

As we help you journey through your Life Change, you will discover how each part of the model is necessary, and how each one supports the others.

In this chapter, we will focus on VISION.

The beginning of a season of transition is to establish your destination. Establishing vision is like typing the destination into your GPS before you begin a journey. Where do you want to land? How will you know when you have arrived?

The word vision is mostly associated with the eyes, or the ability to 'see'. The better you can see, the better your vision. The clearer your vision, the easier it is to plan a pathway to get there. If you are a leader, you may be interested in our leadership programs; they focus on leading organisations and teams to the fulfilment of a clear vision. However, for the Life Change program, we ask the following Questions:

## 1. What Is Your Core Purpose?

Write down your deep why. What is the problem you are on earth to solve? Remember, here is what I wrote above:

> *I believe that my purpose on Earth is to solve the problem of hopelessness and discouragement. I have a deep belief that human beings have the power to live extraordinary lives. I see potential in everyone I meet, and I am driven to help empower people to live to and fulfil that potential.*

Try to write your own purpose statement.

## 2. Who Do You Most Want to Help?

This is an important question. Some people might answer this question with 'everybody'. Of course, we all want to help everybody, but most of us are more effective when we add some focus to our vision. Take, for example, this book. I would like it to be of help to everybody; I think it could help anybody, but mostly I hope it helps people who are experiencing a season of transition in their life.

On a broader scale, as a mentor and coach in the market place, I find that I can't be a coach to everybody. For example, I am not a coach to sports people, I am not a personal trainer, I am not a marriage coach, I am not a school teacher, and I am not a tutor. Mostly, I am a coach and mentor to leaders, and of those leaders, I am best when I stand with those in business.

Take some time to think about who you most want to help. My wife is a Pilates instructor. Anyone can come to her studio, however she mostly wants to help people who have injuries or are experiencing pain.

## Chapter Eight: Keep Your Core Values- Change Your How Not Your Why

Who do you most want to help?

## 3. How Could You Best Help Them?

Consider different ways you could help people. A person who would like to empower young people to succeed may consider being a school teacher, or a youth worker, or a psychologist, or a life coach.

Consider these three questions in the context of my wife's transition:

Her core purpose is to *empower women to live lives of health, wellness, and fulfilment*.

The people she would most want to help are *women between the ages of 40 and 65 years who are experiencing pain or injury*.

Her next question is: *How could she best help them?* If she was early in her Life Change process she may make a list like the following:

- Be a personal trainer
- Train to be a physiotherapist or a chiropractor
- Develop her nursing skills to work in pain management
- Train to be a counsellor
- Learn to teach yoga
- Train in occupational therapy
- Learn to be a nutrition coach or dietician
- Open a Pilates studio

There are many ways to help women between the ages of 40 and 65 years, who are in pain or have an injury, to live a life of health, wellness and fulfilment. Over time, she just had to choose an option. Why did she choose the Pilates Studio? Mostly because it was aligned to her story. At the age of 51 she was experiencing burnout, was in a life transition, and was suffering with chronic back pain from a previous work injury. She attended a Pilates class and over time she journeyed to a place of health, wellness, and fulfilment.

Consider the model below:

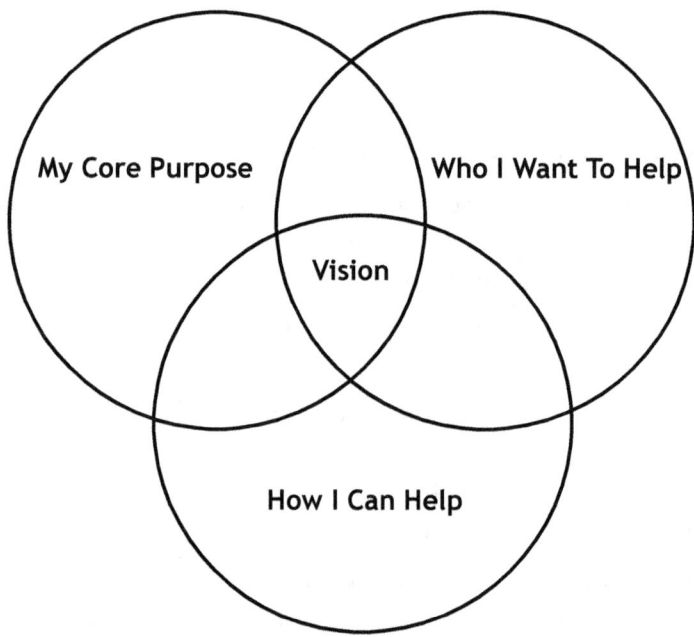

As we transition through our Life Change, our most likely destination will be the overlap of our core purpose, who we want to help, and how we can best help them.

Before you move on, consider filling out the following table:

## Chapter Eight: Keep Your Core Values- Change Your How Not Your Why

| My Core Purpose | Who I want to help | How I can help |
|---|---|---|
|  |  |  |

Once you have filled out the above table, you can write down what we call 'a brief vision statement'. Our definition of a vision statement is a brief description of the outcomes for the person you want to help.

For the Pilates Studio, the vision statement could be:

*Empowering health and wellness to women experiencing pain or injury through Pilates.*

My vision statement could be:

*Building and empowering extraordinary leaders.*

What's yours?

| My Vision Statement |
|---|
|  |

CHAPTER NINE
## Surround the Vision with REST Resource

Clarity around vision is only a first step towards a successful Life Change. There is an ancient text that says, 'The end of a matter is better than its beginning, and patience is better than pride'. Another says, 'One who puts on his armour should not boast like one who takes it off'.

Both texts suggest that having a vision is the easy part, bringing the vision to pass is where we often fall short. The REST model gives a balanced approach to bringing the vision to pass and completing the Life Change transition. In this chapter we will journey through the first of the four sectors:

### RESOURCE

When we think of resource, we are considering whether we have the financial and personal resources to complete the transition.

In our context we had neither, so it was a necessary consideration. Financially we were not in a good place, and emotionally and mentally we had been running on empty for a long time. Although the resource sector of the REST model goes beyond these two considerations, it is these two that we will confine ourselves to in this Life Change book. Let's start with financial resources.

## FINANCIAL RESOURCES

A major life transition is stressful enough on its own without adding financial stress as well. In our 'leverage everything' chapter we wrote of the need to leverage finances. Let's take that a step further. What if you have no savings to leverage, or alternatively, what if you are not of a mind to renovate and rent properties like we did? Quite simply, you need another plan. If you have no plan you will lie awake at night worrying over how you will cover your expenses.

The question is this: How will you pay the bills while you are in transition? I have met people who have transitioned into business with no savings at all. They were dependent upon their first sales to survive. This only caused increased stress and sleepless nights.

Part of the Life Change process is to write down the different cashflow options with a trained mentor in order to build a financial strategy to support the transition.

Consider the following model:

### Chapter Nine: Surround the Vision with REST Resource

| Cashflow Options | Temporary/ Long Term? | Future Financial Return? | Priority |
|---|---|---|---|
|  |  |  |  |

In the first column, write down the different options that could create the required cashflow to see you through your Life Change.

These could include:

- Living off savings
- One partner working
- Both partners working
- Government/social support
- Help from extended family
- Cashing in stocks or investments
- Starting a new business

In the second column write down whether this is a temporary or long-term solution. For example, living off savings is clearly a temporary solution. One partner working may be a long-term solution if the partner is in a vocation they would like to pursue long term.

In the third column, consider the future financial return on each option. For example, cashing in stocks or investments would cause a negative financial return whereas one partner re-entering the workforce could have long term benefits as they become established in a new career.

If a new business or enterprise was started, the future financial returns may be favourable, however there may need to be a short-term plan for cash flow while the business gets established. One option that we chose was to have one partner (myself) earning an income while the other started a new enterprise.

This model changed throughout our transition. In the first stage I worked a full-time job while my wife rested, and I also attended to the property investments. After some time, she started to work part-time, while I dropped back to part time as I began to rest. Eventually, I returned to full-time work while my wife started her new business. All the way through our Life Change we ensured we had a cash flow plan. This ensured finance did not become an additional and unnecessary stress.

In the fourth column, prioritise each option, one being the least attractive, five being the most attractive. This will help you choose your best option going forward.

## PERSONAL RESOURCES

The second consideration in the context of resource is to undertake a measure of your own personal resources. One of the major triggers of our Life Change was my wife's burnout. Today, she is fully recovered, however in 2010 she was very unwell. She could hardly maintain a conversation without stuttering. Tears would flow easily. She was struggling with depression, and any level of social interaction was a major effort for her.

Of course, this needed to be taken into consideration before we embarked on our Life Change. We were confident that she would not always be in this situation, but we also understood that until her mental and emotional tanks were replenished anything high stress was out of the question. Our priority was to fill her tanks again.

For the first three months we did very little except walk the beach and drink coffee. We were able to do this through the kindness of friends who had a beach house they provided for us. Remember the leverage chapter? By that time, I was ready to take on some work, but her tanks were still depleted, so as I took on employment she continued to rest and paint (as an exceptional artist, painting and creativity replenishes her soul).

The point here is to know how to measure your own personal gauges and to ensure that you are not running on empty.

There are many trained specialists who can help you read your gauges however we will include some basic principles that helped us:

## RESOURCE self-analysis

1. On a scale of one to ten, one being empty and ten being full, how full is your emotional tank?
2. On a scale of one to ten, one being exhausted and ten being fully functional, what is the level of your mental energy?
3. What activities deplete your emotional and mental reserves?
4. What activities replenish your emotional and mental reserves?
5. What boundaries can you put in place that will limit those activities that deplete your emotional and mental reserves?
6. What routines and disciplines can you put in place that will ensure you regularly access those activities that replenish you?

The main takeaway from this chapter is to ensure that your financial and personal resources are in place before you embark on your significant Life Change.

CHAPTER TEN
# Surround the Vision with REST Ethos

ONCE WE HAVE considered our financial and personal resources, we turn to Ethos. Most definitions for the word Ethos would include the beliefs, attitudes, and values of a person or community.

Revisiting Ethos is an important part of our Life Change journey because it is often our beliefs and values that send us off course in the first place. As we began our transition we received timely help from a kindly, experienced psychologist who specialized in burn-out. I will not attempt in one chapter to replace the depth of counsel that can been gained from an experienced professional, however I would like to demonstrate how ethos is an important part of the REST model.

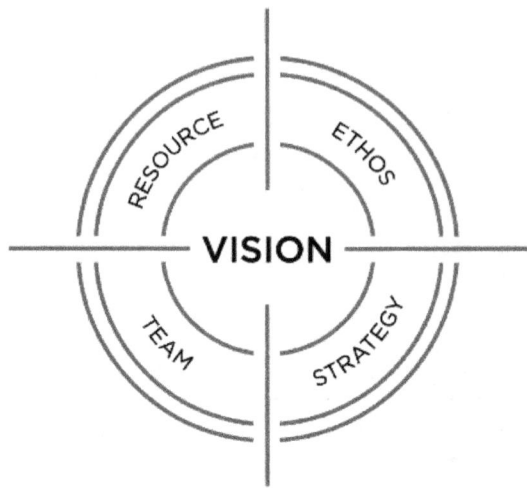

As we transition towards reaching for a new vision, we might have the resources in place, a clear strategy, and the right team around us, *but* if our ethos is unhealthy we can be destined to repeat past mistakes and burn out again.

## UNHEALTHY BELIEFS

A significant part of our journey was to identify and replace the unhealthy beliefs that had caused us pain and failure in the past. The danger of unhealthy beliefs is in the very idea that they are beliefs. If we knew they were unhealthy, we would not believe them. Then there are beliefs we know are unhealthy, but they have become mindsets within us that are difficult to change.

Of course, unhealthy beliefs are unique to the individual who carries them, so my unhealthy beliefs may be very different to those of the reader. But let me share some of the thought patterns we needed to change to successfully transition to a new season. Our unhealthy thought patterns manifested in the form of questions. The questions were like the part of the iceberg than can be seen above the water. It's what lay beneath the questions that needed to be addressed.

## 1. Can I Afford to Let Go of Our Current Income?

This may present as a sensible question, until you consider the consequences of the answer being no. Beneath this question was a mindset of fear and anxiety. If the answer is no, does that mean that we will remain trapped in a lifestyle that has lost its sense of purpose and joy? How many remain trapped in a life they despise because they cannot *afford* to change? This makes us victims of our current circumstances. Of course, a better question would be, how can I afford to let go of our current income? At a deeper level, we would ask a person going through the Life Change program where their questions come from.

## 2. Do I Have What it Takes?

Again, this is a relevant question. Yet it is only relevant if the transition is an impossible one. I am never going to win the hundred meters sprint at the Olympic Games, so if that is the goal of my Life Change the answer is clearly, No, I do not have what it takes.

This is an important distinction to make. Believing we have what it takes to achieve any goal will only end in discouragement. For example, fish will never climb trees, and monkeys will never live in the ocean. Asking them to do so would be asking them to do the impossible.

But it was not the goal of my transition to do the impossible.

Life Change

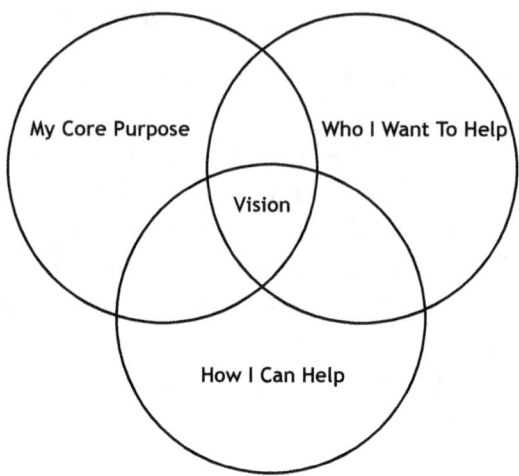

Remember the three circles we drew in chapter eight?

The end goal of your Life Change is to be aligned with your true core purpose, to help a specific group of people, and to do so in a way that reflects your gifts and abilities. In other words, you are transitioning to the life you were born to live. If you were born to live this life, I would suggest that you were also born with the capacity to do so. Anything less is an unhealthy belief.

## 3. Am I Too Old to Start Again?

Surely this was a valid question for us. I remember when I was a teenager thinking that 50 was old! Of course, now that I am 56 my views have changed. Yet this was also a question that exposed an unhealthy belief. Is it ever too late to live the life you were born for? Is it ever too late to change from an unhealthy environment? When is too old? Most of us know of Colonel Sanders who sold his first restaurant at age 65 to build his KFC franchise in earnest, but have you heard of Gladys Burrill who ran her first marathon at age 92, or Peter Mark Roget who published *Roget's Thesaurus of English Words and Phrases* at age 73, or Harry Bernstein who published his first book, *The Invisible Wall: A love story that broke barriers* at age 96?

## 4. What Will People Think?

This was an important question for me, and it did reveal some very unhealthy beliefs that I had to address. I have mentioned my unhealthy relationship with my father. This left me with a tendency to look for the affirmation that was missing when I was growing up; it was important to me to be accepted and admired by those I respected. This unhealthy belief needed to be addressed as I transitioned to a place of healthier self-esteem and the belief that the people who matter will stand with me, and those who don't, don't matter.

## 5. Am I a Failure?

We were letting go of a career before we had fulfilled our goals and dreams. We had believed for so much more; walking away was devastating. Personally, I felt I was a terrible failure. Many of my peers had gone on to live successful lives and careers, yet here we were selling our possessions and leaving town with our dreams in tatters.

## REPLACING UNHEALTHY BELIEFS

We needed to address our feelings of failure, so we could embark on our Life Change journey.

The following table represents the replacements we embraced to our questions:

| Questions | Replacement |
|---|---|
| Can I afford to let go of our current income? | I can make a way to make this work financially. |
| Do I have what it takes? | I was born with the gifts and abilities to live this life. |
| Am I too old to start again? | It's never too late to live the life of your dreams. |
| What will people think? | The people who matter will always think the best of me. If they don't, they don't matter. |
| Am I a failure? | Failure is not getting up when knocked down. Our best days are ahead of us. |

Take some time to consider your questions and the unhealthy thought patterns that lie beneath. For each question, find the replacement that will enable you to be successful in your Life Change.

| Questions | Replacements |
|---|---|
|  |  |
|  |  |
|  |  |
|  |  |
|  |  |

## VALUES

The second part of our Ethos chapter embraces the subject of values. I have always been of the belief that values should be intentional. They are better by choice than by chance; by design as opposed to default.

More recently I have embraced the concept of contextual values. These are sets of values that we embrace for the different areas of our lives. At the beginning of our Life Change journey I followed a process of establishing a set of five values that I would choose to form the foundation of my personal life. They were faith, integrity, generosity, humility and forgiveness. In each situation or decision that I encountered I would ask five questions: What would faith do? What would integrity do? What would generosity do? What would humility do? What would forgiveness do? None of us live the perfect life, however values can help us live better lives.

You may like to choose five personal values and enter them below:

| My Personal Values |
|---|
|  |
|  |
|  |
|  |
|  |

In the context of our Life Change transition, I would encourage you to embrace a second set of values. It is this process that will prepare you for your destination. Let's look again at our three circles:

Life Change

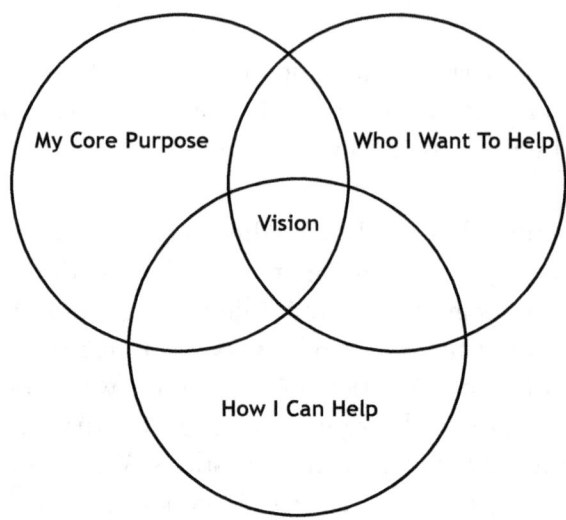

Take some time to review each circle: What is your life purpose? Who do you want to help? How can you help?

Here is how I answered these questions:

## 1. My Core Purpose

*I believe that my purpose on Earth is to solve the problem of hopelessness and discouragement. I have a deep belief that human beings have the power to live extraordinary lives. I see potential in everyone I meet, and I am driven to help empower people to live to and fulfil that potential.*

## 2. Who do I want to help?

*Leaders and business owners.*

## 3. How can I help?

*As a mentor, coach, and author.*

Chapter Ten: Surround the Vision with REST Ethos

Write your answers below:

| | |
|---|---|
| My Core Purpose. | |
| Who do I want to help? | |
| How can I help? | |

Having answered your three questions, consider five to seven values that you could embrace to best live out your answers. For example, after reviewing my three answers I could choose the following values to be the person I will need to be:

Encouragement, Empathy, Empowering, Transparency, and Commitment.

I didn't need to include any of my personal values since they are already embraced.

Write your *vision* values in the first column of the table below:

| My Vision Values | Therefore |
|---|---|
| | |
| | |
| | |
| | |
| | |
| | |
| | |

67

The challenge with values is that many people write down their list and yet nothing in their life changes. Values do not become our culture unless they are regularly acted upon. For this reason we have added a second column headed up *Therefore*. Beside each value, write a sentence beginning with the word *Therefore*.

For example, some of mine may look like this:

Encouragement: Therefore, in every conversation, I will always seek to leave people with greater confidence than when we first met.

Empathy: Therefore, I will always take the time to understand the real pain and frustrations of those I help, never taking them for granted.

Finally, take the time to review your beliefs and values tables. I hope that these exercises are helping you to see that you really can become a better human being as you transition your Life Change.

Ethos, when understood in the context of the REST model, enables us to become the person we need to be to fulfil the vision.

CHAPTER ELEVEN
# Surround the Vision with REST Strategy

STRATEGY TAKES A further look at the *how* behind our *what*. In our Leadership program, we look quite comprehensively at writing a strategic plan for leaders, however in Life Change we need only answer two primary questions:

1. What is the one thing that we *do* in fulfilling our vision as demonstrated in our three circles? We call this our *mission*.
2. What three activities can I be extremely good at in fulfilling the mission?

Before we go further in this chapter it may be wise for me to make an observation. Building your strategy for the future may not be something you attempt at the beginning of your Life Change process. In the early days of our Life Change, my only strategy was to survive. It wasn't until we were somewhat replenished that a strategy for the future became important. Now let's move on.

## MISSION

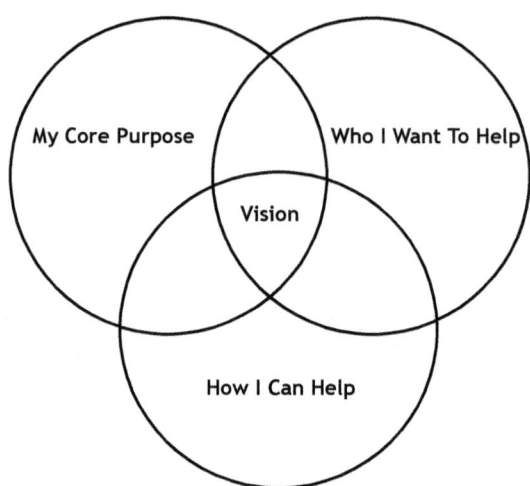

Let's begin by again reviewing the three circles:

From my three circles, I was able to identify that my vision is to encourage and empower leaders and business owners to succeed by being a mentor and coach. From that discovery, I was able to write a mission statement that went something like this:

*To produce and deliver outstanding leadership and business resources that lift leaders to their highest potential.*

Although the above statement looks easy to write, in practice it takes weeks, and sometimes months, to get it right. In fact, even the statement above may further change and adapt until it is something I believe best reflects my mission.

## WRITE YOUR MISSION

Consider your three circles and write a mission statement below. A key to help you with this statement is to include an action (what you do) and a result (the outcome of what you do). For example, my mission statement is:

*To produce and deliver outstanding leadership and business resources (Action) that lift leaders to their highest potential (Result).*

---

My mission is:

---

## STRATEGY

Once we have identified our mission, we move to our second question:

What three activities can I be extremely good at in fulfilling my mission? This is what we call a strategy statement. It is focusing all the many activities that you *could* adopt into three activities that you can be outstanding at. Our Pilates Studio mission statement may be:

*To provide a Pilates Studio with all the necessary resources (Action) to enable our clients to be healthy; body, mind and spirit (Result).*

Having established the mission, we could choose three activities that we can be outstanding at. Therefore, the strategy statement may be:

*To be remarkable in the studio we provide, the classes we offer, and the community we create.*

These are three activities that we can become very good at, and in so doing fulfil the mission.

We can discover our strategy statement by overlapping two questions:

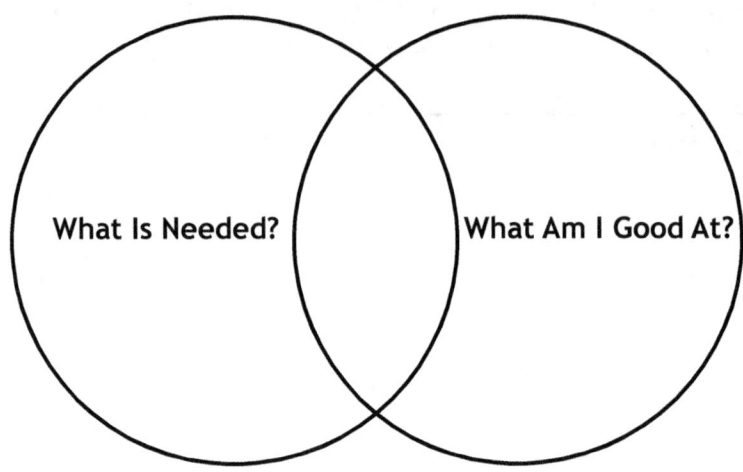

Our three activities need to be both something we can be extremely good at, and also something that is needed by those we intend to help.

As an example, in my Life Change process I chose my mission statement to be:

*To produce and deliver outstanding leadership and business resources that lift leaders to their highest potential.*

If I could be successful in my mission, I would fulfil my vision of:

*Building extraordinary leaders.*

Next, I needed to choose three activities that I could be outstanding at. Looking back at my career so far, I could see three areas that I have a proven record in being good at: strategy, content, and delivery.

Strategy: I have a naturally strategic mind. I love to help people create a strategic plan to bring a vision or goal to pass. I asked myself, 'What if I could become outstanding as a business and leadership strategist?' I may not be able to be great at everything, but I could become great at that one thing.

Content: I love to write content. I have given 5000+ presentations over my thirty-year career, and I have seldom repeated the same content. I like the process of being creative. I love producing original work. What if I could become outstanding in producing content that helps leaders become extraordinary?

Delivery: As mentioned, I have presented 5000+ times, mainly as a keynote speaker, but also as a workshop facilitator. Mostly, the feedback has been positive. But what if I could develop my delivery skills in such a way as to become outstanding?

By choosing these three activities to become my focus, I was able to write a strategy statement:

*To be outstanding in the content I create, the delivery of that content, and in helping leaders create strategies for success.*

Here is how I filled in the two circles:

Consider your history so far. What three activities can you become outstanding at that will also help the people you would like to serve? Write your strategy statement below:

> My strategy is:

As an example, my two statements look like this:

> My mission is:
>
> To produce and deliver outstanding leadership and business resources that lift leaders to their highest potential.

## Chapter Eleven: Surround the Vision with REST Strategy

> My strategy is:
>
> To be outstanding in the content I create, the delivery of that content, and in helping leaders create strategies for success.

Mission and strategy statements give a very clear definition of what you will be doing when you arrive at the destination of your Life Change journey.

In my work-life, I can now regularly ask two questions:

1. Am I lifting leaders to their highest potential through the resources I both produce and deliver?
2. Does everything I do fall within the categories of creating content, delivering that content, and creating strategies for success?

I can answer yes to both questions. And if the answer is no, I need to either adjust what I am doing, or adjust the statements.

# CHAPTER TWELVE
## Surround the Vision with REST Team

Our final chapter explores one of the most important aspects of the Life Change journey. Quite simply, we should never travel alone. At every stage of our journey we should be able to answer the question: who is travelling with me?

As mentioned before, the REST model is a foundation that we use for several programs. In our Leadership program, team is seen in a strategic and organizational context. However, in our Life Change program the context is the personal journey.

In an earlier chapter we shared that we need to leverage our relationships as we journey through our transition. Taking that thought a step further, we recognised that there were different types of relationships that helped us through our season. The sum-total of those relationships became our very own Life Change team. We invite you to take an inventory through our team members and encourage you to position the people around you who will form your team.

## FAMILY

From our perspective, family was, and remains, the core of our Life Change team. Our transition included some of the most painful moments of our lives. There were some great successes, and some devastating failures. When we get family right, there is no judgment, and love is unconditional.

I have often heard it said that it is in the hardest of times that we find out who our true friends are. I disagree. Many of our closest friends were absent in some of our most difficult moments. Some were unaware of the depth of our pain. Others didn't know what to say or do. Still others were busy with their own battles. And yes, some disagreed with our actions and parted company with us. However, in our eyes they all remain our friends. We would never place our own needy expectations on their shoulders. That is not what friends are for. We love the fact that we have friends who colour our world and enable us to feel normal. We have no expectations that they should be more than great friends. Their every word of encouragement is a bonus, unexpected, and warms our heart.

What we did find, however, is who our family is. Our family stood at our side as a pillar of support and carried a belief in us that kept us sane. They believed in us, cried with us, encouraged us, and celebrated with us.

Keep your family close, let go of offences quickly, and nurture the family relationships that were born for eternity.

## MENTORS AND COACHES

Secondly, we need people who can help us build a road-map to our new destination. One of the reasons this book is being written is that I wish I had the information within it seven years ago.

One of our challenges was not what we didn't know, but that we didn't know what we didn't know!

Make sure you have a mentor or coach in your world during this season. It might cost you some money, but it may save you years.

## PASTORAL CARE AND COUNSELLORS

This is such an important category. A significant Life Change is a very vulnerable season. For some, their Life Change has been forced upon them: the death of a spouse, redundancy, bankruptcy, the failure of a relationship, or a health crisis.

One thing every transition has in common is that these seasons can bring out both the best and the worst in us. Those who offer pastoral care and counselling are not there to help you with the roadmap, but to help traverse how you feel and think along the journey.

I am so thankful for the wise counsellors who accompanied us on our journey. We would not have made it without them.

## EMPLOYERS

If your Life Change includes working for an employer, ensure that you nurture that relationship. I was privileged to connect with a great boss who was already doing many of the things I was interested in.

He was already passionately pursuing a dream of empowering business owners and leaders with all the necessary resources to prosper. I was able to run in the slipstream of his momentum. One principle that I believe is important in our employer relationships is the principle of separation.

You may be experiencing a significant life transition, however, when at work, work! My boss was pursuing his own dream, and he was employing me to help him get there. My advice is to work hard and avoid making your employer your counsellor. He or she may have every desire to help you, but combining these relationships rarely works well.

By keeping your work and personal life separate, you are also giving yourself another world where you can escape to, and where you are not brooding on the challenges of change.

## FRIENDS TO LAUGH AND CRY WITH

Friends often become the colour within our Life Change picture. As mentioned earlier in this chapter, be careful of the expectations you place upon them. They are not your counsellor, your doctor, or your pastor. They are your friends!

They exist for friendship, laughter, drinking coffee, playing golf, going fishing, and generally to help you enjoy the journey. Be to them what you are looking for from them. You will always reap what you sow.

## NETWORKING

Finally, throughout your Life Change journey, network, network, network. I am amazed by the opportunities that have come my way through networking. Everyone you know or meet has an insight, a connection, or an opportunity that may help you on your journey.

I connected with an old acquaintance, who introduced me to his friend, who introduced me to a colleague, who asked me to consult with a training organisation, who then asked me to head their business school, which opened doors to a group of leaders, who connected me with an opportunity to speak across a whole nation. All from one phone call.

## TAKING ACTION

One of the temptations when going through a significant Life Change is to withdraw and become isolated. Please don't do that. Get out and about. Go to meetings, attend seminars and conferences, and say yes to invitations. You never know who you will meet who can open your next door of opportunity.

As we close out our final chapter, may I encourage you in this way; embrace the principles within the REST model. Be clear in your vision, build your resources, establish your ethos, have a strategy, and gather your team. The future is filled with hope and opportunity. Your best is yet to come.

# EPILOGUE
## Transition Versus Change

BEFORE WE DRAW to a close, let's finish with a final word of wisdom. There is a vast difference between the principles of transition and change. Change is playing the short game. You decide to change, and you change. Whereas transition is a process. It is playing the long game.

Our journey began with a sudden change; however it then became a long process of transition. Take your time. There is no rush.

One way to understand this difference is that change is an event, while transition is a process. Change is often external, while transition is often internal.

Our world changed when we decided to resign from our position. But we then needed to understand that the change in itself was not the destination. It was only the beginning of a journey that would take time and process to complete. Let me finish by offering five key principles of transition that will help you through your Life Change journey.

## 1. Contentment is in the Journey Not the Destination

Avoid believing that you will be happy when you arrive at your destination. Be happy in the now. Change is coming, but not to make you happy. Change is simply a journey that happy people traverse.

## 2. Keep Resetting the GPS

Early in our transition I had a general idea of where I thought we would land. However, many doors closed and our circumstances changed over time. The destination that I had typed into our GPS became both unrealistic and even at times, undesirable. Often, we felt lost, like we had turned corners only to find that the road came to a dead-end.

Over time I decided to set early Monday mornings aside to review, and at times reset the vision. Most times we stayed the course, but through this habit of weekly review, the future became increasingly clear.

With a significant Life Change, we can begin lost, or have a vague idea of the future, and we find clarity on the way. Don't be afraid of resetting the destination in the GPS.

## 3. Stop for Refreshments

The Life Change journey can be an intense and stressful experience. Often over our married life we enjoyed motorcycling. We would love the journey, but it wouldn't be too long before a certain part of our anatomy would feel the effects of sitting too long. Perhaps we needed a more comfortable seat.

To avoid the discomfort, we learned to schedule regular stops for refreshments. The same applies to our Life Change journey. Schedule your stops for refreshment. Plan a weekend away, day trips, or Saturday mornings at your favourite café for breakfast.

We landed in Melbourne, Australia. Melbourne is known for its many excellent cafes. For the first six months we spent every Saturday morning having breakfast at a different café. We would search online for best or favourite cafes, and stop for refreshments each week, drinking coffee, reading the paper, and often walking the beaches.

Stopping for refreshments is best undertaken intentionally. Schedule your stops, think about what will replenish you, and make sure life doesn't become such a rush that you just keep riding to the destination.

## 4. Check Your Passengers

Remember that you are not travelling alone. When our family was much younger, our oldest child was prone to car sickness. If we drove on windy roads it wouldn't take long before he would become pale, and if we didn't stop quickly the car would be sprayed with vomit. Unpleasant to say the least.

The fact is, traveling windy roads can cause those traveling with you to become unwell. We soon made it a habit of watching out for him. We would often ask, "How are you feeling?" "Are you okay?" "Would you like to take a break?"

Consider those who are traveling with you. What is the effect on them of your Life Change? Consider whether you need to ask the questions above.

How are you feeling?

Are you okay?

Would you like to take a break?

## 5. Travel Rested

My original purpose in developing the REST model was to establish a pattern of leadership where a leader could rest easy on the journey. If the vision is clear, the resources are in place, ethos is healthy, a good strategy has been designed, and the right people are on the team, a leader can sleep easy at night and minimize the risks of burnout.

The same principle applies to those on a Life Change journey. Trust the transition process and learn to rest easy. Avoid emotions like guilt and depression, don't be impatient, and most of all, believe that transition does not mean failure.

My sense of failure almost overwhelmed me. As a man I wanted to be a good provider for my family, and to find a level of success that would leave a legacy for future generations. My resignation brought my world crashing around me. As I finally eased into our transition I learnt to believe that the doors that closed were repositioning me for a new season. I learned the discipline of traveling rested.

Let me leave you with this final thought: It is neither the journey, nor the destination that defines you. In the end, how you loved is all that matters. Love God, love others, and love yourself. Embrace this and you will find that wherever you are in your Life Change journey, you have already arrived at what matters.

www.ingramcontent.com/pod-product-compliance
Lightning Source LLC
Chambersburg PA
CBHW050604300426
44112CB00013B/2069